Earn. Save. Give.

Youth Study Book

Earn. Save. Give.
Wesley's Simple Rules for Money

Earn. Save. Give.
978-1-63088-392-8
978-1-63088-393-5 eBook

Earn. Save. Give. - Large Print Edition
978-1-63088-394-2

Earn. Save. Give. - Leader Guide
978-1-63088-395-9
978-1-63088-396-6 eBook

Earn. Save. Give. - DVD
978-1-63088-397-3

Earn. Save. Give. - Program Guide
978-1-63088-398-0 Flash Drive
978-1-63088-399-7 Download

Earn. Save. Give. - Youth Study Book
978-1-63088-400-0
978-1-63088-401-7 eBook

Earn. Save. Give. - Children's Leader Guide
978-1-63088-402-4

Earn. Save. Give. - Devotional Readings for Home
978-1-5018-0507-3
978-1-5018-0509-7 Package of 25
978-1-5018-0508-0 eBook

For more information, visit www.AbingdonPress.com.

Also by James A. Harnish

A Disciple's Heart

A Disciple's Path

Believe in Me

Converge Bible Studies:
Women of the Bible

Journey to the Center of the Faith

Living with the Mind of Christ

Passion, Power, and Praise

Radical Renovation

reConnect

Rejoicing in Hope

Simple Rules for Money

Strength for the Broken Places

You Only Have to Die

JAMES A. HARNISH

Wesley's Simple Rules
for Money

YOUTH STUDY BOOK
by Josh Tinley

Abingdon Press / Nashville

EARN. SAVE. GIVE.
Wesley's Simple Rules for Money

Youth Study Book
by Josh Tinley

This book is printed on elemental chlorine-free paper.
ISBN 978-1-63088-400-0

15 16 17 18 19 20 21 22 23 24—10 9 8 7 6 5 4 3 2 1
MANUFACTURED IN THE UNITED STATES OF AMERICA

Contents

Introduction
Get on the John Wesley Financial Plan

If you've spent much time in a church that has *Methodist* or *Wesleyan* as part of its name, you've probably heard the name John Wesley. If you haven't, you're about to find out about him, and I think you'll be delighted and inspired.

John Wesley, through his teachings and the example of his life, had an influence on dozens of Christian denominations and traditions, including The United Methodist Church, the Church of the Nazarene, the African Methodist Episcopal Church, Churches of God, and the Salvation Army. The funny thing is that Wesley didn't set out to start a new denomination; he just wanted to be a better Christian.

Those who were influenced by Wesley's teaching and example called themselves *Methodists*, a term originally coined to poke fun at John Wesley's methodical approach to faith. Wesley's hope was for Methodism to be a revival movement within the Church of England; he never intended for there to be a separate Methodist Church. Nonetheless, those who called themselves Methodists looked to

Wesley for wisdom and guidance on a host of subjects, including their finances.

John Wesley had plenty to say about money. Throughout his pastoral career he ministered mostly to people who subsisted on meager incomes, struggling to meet their basic needs. But as the Methodist movement grew, and as those who took Wesley's teachings to heart saw their financial situation improve, he became a pastor to the affluent as well. Wesley didn't discriminate when it came to teaching the faithful how to manage their funds. He held the poor and the wealthy to similar standards and suggested that all God's people—regardless of salary—adhere to three financial rules:

- Earn all you can.
- Save all you can.
- Give all you can.

(Actually, instead of "earn all you can," Wesley said "gain all you can." But the word *earn* has more meaning to us today, so that's the one we'll use.)

While Wesley's three rules are concise and easy to remember, they are grounded in biblical wisdom and Christian tradition and have been tested by Wesley himself, as well as by many of his spiritual descendants. Living by these rules requires us to put aside greed and selfishness and to focus on God's purposes. When followed, these rules will equip us to use our money and resources generously in service of God and God's people.

Now Is the Time to Develop Holy Habits

Often when church leaders address giving, stewardship, and other money-related issues, they do so with adults in mind. As a young person, you might not be able to relate to a sermon directed toward people who have bills to pay and debts to manage. You might not yet have experienced the joy of receiving a regular paycheck or the stress that comes with figuring out how far it will go. But even if you've never had to file taxes or make a big financial decision, you can benefit from John Wesley's three rules for money.

In this study, you will consider what it means—for you at this time in your life—to earn, to save, and to give. You will reflect on how you can make faithful use not only of money but of all the other resources that God has entrusted you with. The hope is that you will get into the habit of making wise and faithful use of your God-given gifts now and that these habits will still be with you years from now when you find yourself with a mortgage and a 401K retirement account.

As you work through this Youth Study Book of *Earn. Save. Give.*, consider what you can start doing or doing differently with your money and resources now. It's impossible to foresee what the future has in store for you and your finances, but you can face the coming days with confidence, knowing that God's wisdom influences all your monetary decisions.

Using This Resource

This book is designed as a group study but also can be used for personal reading and devotion. Each session begins with a chapter for group members or individuals to read. Persons using this study can read these chapters on their own or can set aside time for personal reading during their group meetings.

Sessions also include a variety of activities and discussion prompts for groups. Some involve reading and discussion; others involve tasks and projects that will require follow-up. Many activities refer to particular sections in the chapter. It may be beneficial to read aloud the corresponding sections while you are working on an activity.

Several activities invite participants to reflect on and discuss personal goals, feelings, and experiences with a partner or small group. It is essential that all participants in this study treat their fellow participants with love and respect. Any personal information that becomes known during discussion should be treated as confidential and received without judgment.

Enjoy this time you have to learn and reflect on wise and faithful financial decisions. Cherish the insight you gain, not only from Scripture and church tradition but also from your friends and peers. Most importantly, consider how you can respond to what you learn and begin developing holy habits when it comes to managing your money and resources.

1.
We Don't Need More Money; We Need Wisdom

1. We Don't Need More Money; We Need Wisdom

Happy are those who find wisdom
and those who gain understanding.
Her profit is better than silver,
and her gain better than gold.
—Proverbs 3:13-14

A Wise and Discerning Mind

Do you remember the first time you were given money? Maybe you received a small weekly allowance; maybe you earned money for completing chores or getting good grades. What did you do with that money? Did you keep it, hoping that you'd soon be able to add to your total? Did you spend it right away on something you'd had your eye on? How did you decide what you'd do with your newly acquired wealth?

Now think back to the first time you made a decision that you regretted involving money. Perhaps you emptied your piggy bank for something you didn't really need. Perhaps you purchased an item that turned out to be flimsy and was broken or useless within a few weeks. Perhaps you received a crisp $20 bill as a gift, and instead of saving it or using it to buy something nice, you spent it on little things like candy and soda.

You may have heard the expression, "A fool and his money are soon parted." This saying, which originated in Dr. John Bridges' 1587 book, *Defence of the Government of the Church of England in Ecclesiastical Matters*, suggests a relationship between wisdom and financial well-being. It seems obvious that one who is wise will fare better financially than one who is foolish. But what, exactly, is wisdom? We often use wise as a synonym for smart, but wisdom is much more than knowledge or even intelligence. People who are wise are not only knowledgeable of what is right and true and just, but they also use good judgment and discernment.

The Bible has plenty to say about wisdom. The Old Testament contains a collection of wisdom literature including the books of Ecclesiastes, Song of Solomon, and Proverbs. Most of the writing in these books is attributed to King Solomon, the son of King David and one of the rulers during ancient Israel's golden age—although many of the Bible's wise sayings likely had been passed down among the Hebrew people for centuries before that. First Kings 3 tells us that shortly after Solomon assumed the throne, God appeared to him in a dream and said, "Ask whatever you wish, and I'll give it to you" (1 Kings 3:5). Instead of asking for a great army, expanded territory, or anything else that may have been useful for a young ruler wanting to establish himself, Solomon asked for wisdom: "Please give your servant a discerning mind in order to govern your people and to distinguish good from evil" (1 Kings 3:9). We too should strive to have a wise and discerning mind in all that we do.

Reverence, Humility, and, uh, Fear?

As a species, we human beings are pretty clever. We've created, discovered, and accomplished so many amazing things that it's easy for us to get a big head and forget the source of our knowledge and creativity. Proverbs 3:5 says, "Trust in the Lord with all your heart; / don't rely on your own intelligence." This is not to say that we shouldn't value our intelligence or that we shouldn't strive to be wise. Rather, it means that we need to keep things in perspective.

To help us keep things in perspective, Proverbs tells us that wisdom begins with "fear of the Lord" (Proverbs 1:7 and 9:10). The idea that God is someone we should fear may seem contrary to what we know about God through Jesus and the Holy Spirit. We know God as a companion, advocate, teacher, and friend. God isn't someone who should frighten us.

Actually, the word *fear* isn't a perfect translation of what the Bible is talking about. A word such as *revere* or *respect* may be more accurate. But it's important that we not lose the "bite" that comes with *fear*. Fear gets our attention; it shakes us up; it forces us to respond. Often in Scripture when human beings find themselves in God's presence, their first instinct is to be afraid. Frequently God's messengers open their messages to God's people by saying, "Do not be afraid." Something about God's presence causes people to tremble.

A healthy fear of God is not a fear that causes us to freak out; it is a fear that acknowledges the power, majesty, and magnitude of the God we serve. It is a fear that keeps us humble and reminds us that we are human, with limits and shortcomings. God, by contrast, is infinite, eternal, and all-knowing. As we strive to be wise with our money, or with anything else, we must look with hope toward the source of all wisdom.

Three Plain Little Rules

John Wesley, the influential eighteenth-century clergyman and theologian and the founder of Methodism, ministered during a turbulent time in England. The disparity between the wealthy and the poor was stark, and violence was rampant. Methodism began, not as a denomination or church, but as a revival movement. Wesley and the early Methodists were interested in transforming the Church of England and England as a whole. This included improving the financial situation of the country's poorest people and holding the richest accountable for how they used their wealth.

Wesley understood the power of money to corrupt and destroy, but he also recognized its power to do good. And he knew that money was a primary concern for the people he ministered to. Those who were of modest means had to manage their money carefully; those who were well off had to avoid being self-serving with their income. There were plenty of early Methodists who had gone from poverty to affluence and who had to learn how to handle their newfound riches.

To help the early Methodists use their money in ways that were wise, honored God, and were beneficial to God's people, Wesley introduced "three plain rules" for the use of money:

- Gain (earn) all you can.
- Save all you can.
- Give all you can.

Simple, right?

Though memorizing these three rules is easy, following them is more challenging. Wesley introduced these maxims in his sermon, "The Use of Money," but he referred to them in many other sermons. Each rule complements the teaching of Scripture and the witness of the church.

Throughout this study, you will consider these three rules as you reflect on your personal experience with money and as you study what the Bible has to say on the subject. Along the way, you'll learn a bit about managing your money wisely and for God's glory.

Session 1 Activities

Just One Wish
Supplies: A Bible

Imagine that an angel walks in on your group and, because you have been so devoted to learning and growing as a faithful Christian community, the angel grants each one of you one wish. What would you ask for?

Give everyone a few minutes to think of a wish, then have all the group members say what they would wish for. Discuss the benefits and drawbacks of each request. For instance, if someone wished for a large sum of money, how could he or she use that money for good? On the other hand, what might be some negative side effects of having lots of money?

After talking about everyone's wishes, read 1 Kings 3:4-14.

- What did Solomon request from God?
- How did God respond?
- What are the potential benefits of Solomon's wish?
- Are there any potential drawbacks or negative side effects to Solomon's request?
- What does this Scripture teach about the value of God's wisdom?

Read "A Wise and Discerning Mind" from the chapter above. Discuss:

- What is *wisdom*? How is it different from *knowledge* or *intelligence*?

Don't Rely on Your Own Intelligence
Supplies: A markerboard or large sheet of paper and markers

Each person in the group should come up with a list of five accomplishments in human history that they consider most impressive. These could be anything from landing on the moon to building the pyramids to founding nations where people have a say in government to accessing a library's worth of information through a device that fits into our pockets.

After everyone has come up with their ideas, ask the group members to read their lists aloud, then record all their ideas on a markerboard or large sheet of paper. As a group, come to an agreement on which five accomplishments are most impressive.

Human beings have done some pretty amazing things during our time on earth. We've acquired an impressive knowledge and understanding of our world and universe; and we've developed a host of technological wonders. Yet Proverbs tells us that, as human beings, we should not "rely on [our] own intelligence" (3:5).

Read the entirety of Proverbs 3:5-7. Discuss:

- These verses from Proverbs don't say anything negative about human intelligence, and yet we are cautioned not to rely on it. Why do you think that's so?
- How can relying on our own intelligence keep us from trusting fully in God?
- What might be the downside of trusting in our own intelligence when it comes to money?

Get Wise With Your Money

Supplies: A few note cards or card-sized pieces of paper for each person, two standard dice

Everyone should take four or five note cards or card-sized pieces of paper. On each card, group members should write one way that young people might use their money (for example, "Put the money in a savings account" or "Spend the money one dollar at a time in snack machines"). Gather the cards, shuffle them, and place the deck face down.

Select one person to start. That person should roll the dice. The total of the two dice, multiplied by ten, will represent how much money is available. (If the number is 8, that person has $80; if the number is 11, that person has $110; and so on.) The person will then draw a card saying how the money will be used. Next, the entire group will vote on whether using the money in this manner would be wise or foolish. If the group votes "wise," the player keeps the money; if the group votes "foolish," the player loses the money. Keep track, on a whiteboard or sheet of paper, of how much money each person acquires or loses.

After everyone has had a turn, discuss what made the "wise" uses of money wise and what made the "foolish" uses of money foolish. Talk about whether members of the group have had personal experiences with money similar to those on the cards. If so, do they agree with the group's wise-or-foolish judgment?

Play a few rounds, stopping after each to debrief. When you're done, declare a winner. (Be sure to remind the group that winning and losing in this particular game is a product of luck—the card shuffle—and the votes of the other players.) Then discuss:

- How do you determine whether a use of money is wise or foolish?

Read each of the following Scriptures. After each Scripture is read, discuss what it says about our attitude and approach toward money.

- Matthew 25:14-30 (parable of the talents, or valuable coins)
- Luke 12:13-21 (parable of the rich fool)
- Philippians 4:12-13

Money Rules
Supplies: A markerboard or large sheet of paper

As a group, brainstorm some rules for making wise use of money. These rules might involve how we earn money, how we should spend money, or how much money we should save or give away.

After brainstorming, try to pare down your list to five or fewer rules. Then read "Three Plain Little Rules" from the chapter above.

- What were John Wesley's three rules for the use of money?
- How do his rules compare with yours?

In future sessions, we will look at each of Wesley's rules in detail. Until then, make a goal, based on one of your group's rules or one of Wesley's, for how you will use your money. Be specific about your goal and be sure to select a goal that can be met in the coming week. For instance, if you will be getting an allowance or a paycheck in the coming week, you could make a goal involving what portion of that money you could save or give; if you have a habit of buying little things that you don't really need, you could make a goal of going one week without making unnecessary purchases.

Pair off. Tell your goal to your partner. During the week, check in with each other about whether you have successfully kept your goal or are making progress toward your goal.

Close your time together in prayer, asking God for the wisdom to trust in God—and not to rely on your own intelligence—especially when it comes to how you use your money.

2.
Earn All You Can

2. Earn All You Can

Laziness brings poverty;
hard work makes one rich.
—Proverbs 10:4

Surprise!

Have you ever been surprised by something that a preacher said, either in a sermon or in conversation? Perhaps you learned that your 52-year-old pastor enjoyed listening to hip hop; or that she spent several years as a detective before entering the ministry. Or a pastor may have introduced you to a new interpretation of a Scripture that you thought had one clear and obvious meaning. Or maybe you found out for the first time that faithful Christians disagree on a hot-button issue that you had assumed was one-sided. As God's people, we need things to surprise us and challenge our understandings from time to time. Otherwise our faith becomes stale, and we take God's wisdom for granted.

John Wesley likely surprised plenty of people when he preached his sermon on the use of money. Many in his audience would have grown up learning about the dangers of money. Wealth can tempt us and warp our priorities. It can do considerable harm to those who are vulnerable. Jesus lifted up the poor widow who donated all of her savings to the temple treasury; he challenged a rich man to sell his possessions and give away the money he made; he taught that we can't serve God and wealth. Wesley himself was known for being frugal. Those listening to him preach probably would have expected him to present a negative view of money and would have been taken aback when he named his first rule for money: "Gain [earn] all you can." They may have been shocked to hear him go on to say that money is "an excellent gift of God."

You may have heard that the Bible says, "Money is the root of all evil." But it doesn't say that—not exactly, anyway. In his First Letter to Timothy, Paul writes, "People…trying to get rich fall into temptation. They are trapped by many stupid and harmful passions that plunge people into ruin and destruction. The love of money is the root of all kinds of evil" (1 Timothy 6:9-10).

In other words, money, in and of itself, is not evil; but our attitude toward money can be. It's fine to make money, but making money should never be our top priority. It should never control us; we should control it. John Wesley understood that, with the correct attitude and perspective, money could be a tremendous asset.

Work Hard, Gain Money

Wesley's first plain rule for the use of money is "Gain [earn] all you can." Let's look at the full text of his statement: "Gain all you can by honest industry. Use all possible diligence in your calling."[1] We see this same emphasis on working hard throughout the Bible's wisdom literature. Ecclesiastes 3:13, for instance, says, "Moreover, this is the gift of God: that all people should…enjoy the results of their hard work."

The Book of Proverbs frequently contrasts the results of hard work with the results of laziness. Proverbs 14:23 tells us, "There is profit in hard work, / but mere talk leads to poverty," and Proverbs 13:4 points out, "The lazy have strong desires but receive nothing; / the appetite of the diligent is satisfied."

We know that wisdom comes from God. Proverbs 6:6-9 tells us that we can see this divine wisdom at work in the example of the ant:

> Go to the ant, you lazy person;
>> observe its ways and grow wise
> The ant has no commander, officer, or ruler.
>> Even so, it gets its food in summer;
>> gathers its provisions at harvest.
> How long, lazy person, will you lie down?
>> When will you rise from your sleep?

Wesley's first rule mentions one's "calling." We are not to work hard for the sake of working hard but to fulfill the purpose that God has set before us. Often in the church, we use *calling* when talking about how clergy and other church leaders are "called" to serve God as a profession. But every follower of Christ has a calling, even if that calling doesn't involve going into ordained ministry or working full-time in the church.

Some Christians are called to be teachers or lawyers or healthcare professionals. Some are called to run businesses. Some are called to do work that is unheralded and overlooked but nonetheless necessary for society to function. Our calling isn't a matter of salary. In fact, many Christians do unpaid work to support family members who are wage earners. Rather, God calls us to do work that honors God and benefits humankind.

When we are diligent in doing the work that God calls us to do, we will earn money, or our families will earn money; and, as John Wesley teaches us, earning money is a good thing. Acquiring money by honest means will give us even more opportunities to do God's good work.

Hard Work Has Limits

One common TV and movie situation is characters who are so consumed by their work that they have no time left for loved ones. These workaholics earn money by "honest industry," yet they often are portrayed in a negative light. They often are shown as the villains because their priorities are out of whack.

In Luke 10:38-42, Jesus visits a family in Bethany, just outside of Jerusalem. One of his hosts, Martha, is so invested in working hard and making sure that everything is perfect for her honored guest that she neglects to spend time with him. Though Martha wasn't working to earn money, she allowed her work to get in the way of something more important. That something was Jesus.

It is all fine and good to work hard and gain money, but we need limits. Proverbs 23:4 says, "Don't wear yourself out trying to get rich; / be smart enough to stop." If we aren't smart enough to stop, an obsession with hard work and earning money can have negative effects on our relationships with family and friends, on our health, and on our faith. God commands us to take a break from our labor and to make time for rest, recovery, and worship: "Six days you may work and do all your tasks, but the seventh day is a Sabbath to the LORD your God. Do not do any work on it" (Exodus 20:9-10).

It's easy to get the impression that the Bible is anti-money. But money, in and of itself, isn't bad. Money is a resource that we can use to do God's work, and for that reason we should strive to earn money. We just have to know our limits. Jesus taught that we "cannot serve God and wealth" (Matthew 6:24). The good news is that we can use our wealth to serve God. But when making money becomes our primary goal, we need to re-examine our priorities.

Session 2 Activities

Check In

During the first session, you made a goal for using money during the coming week and revealed that goal to a partner. Talk to that partner about whether you met that goal during the week and, if not, what kept you from meeting it.

Rule Number One

Read or reread "Work Hard, Gain Money," in the chapter above. You'll see that John Wesley's first rule for using money is, in its entirety, "Gain all you can by honest industry. Use all possible diligence in your calling."

As mentioned in the chapter, the word *calling* is important. In the church we often use *calling* when talking about clergy and other church leaders, but every follower of Christ has a calling. God calls all of us to use our gifts, talents, and opportunities to accomplish God's purposes.

Think about the career you would most like to go into (or that you are planning on going into). Then, silently, answer these questions:

- What do you know about the amount of money you can expect to make from this career?
- How will you be able to serve God and others through this career?
- On a scale from one to ten (with one being "not important at all" and ten being "extremely important"), how important is salary to your choice of profession?

- On a scale from one to ten, how important is having an opportunity to serve God and others to your choice of profession?

No one needs to reveal their answers to these questions. Instead, discuss how influential each factor—salary or opportunity to serve—*should* be when it comes to making career decisions.

After this activity, you may be under the impression that for you to have the "right" answer, your number for serving God and others should be higher than your number for earning a salary. But it's not that simple.

John Wesley told those in his churches, "Gain all you can." In other words, "Go ahead and make money." While making money shouldn't be our primary aim in life, it is okay—and even good—to earn money. Furthermore, the goals of making money and doing God's work aren't mutually exclusive. We can use the money that we earn to accomplish God's purposes.

"Go to the Ant"
Supplies: Bibles, paper or a markerboard, construction paper or cardstock, markers or colored pencils

Wesley taught that we should gain what we can by "honest industry" or hard work. Read Proverbs 6:6-11. These verses lift up the ant as a creature with an admirable work ethic. As a group, rewrite these verses using a different example, other than an ant. You might choose another animal, or you may choose a person.

Draft your rewrite on a markerboard or a scrap of paper. Then write it nicely on a sheet of construction paper or cardstock. Illustrate your version of Proverbs 6:6-11 with pictures. Display the finished product in your meeting space.

If you have a large group, divide into smaller groups of four or five; each group should do its own rendering of these verses. As you work, talk about hard work:

- What does it mean to work hard? How do you know if you're working hard?
- Who in your life exemplifies hard work? What have you learned from their example?
- Why do you think the Bible speaks so highly of hard work? Why does working hard matter to God?

Match the Proverbs
Supplies: A Bible

Below are four Proverbs, each of which has been split into two parts. Working with a partner or small group, try to correctly match the two parts of each Proverb. Use a Bible to check your answers. Note that the exact phrasing of each proverb may vary, depending on the Bible translation you use. The verses are: Proverbs 12:27; 13:4; 14:23; 19:15.

The lazy don't roast their prey,	the appetite of the diligent is satisfied.
The lazy have strong desires but receive nothing;	a slacker goes hungry.
There is profit in hard work,	but hard workers receive precious riches.
Laziness brings on deep sleep;	but mere talk leads to poverty.

After you've put these Proverbs together, discuss:

- What lesson do these verses teach about the value of hard work?
- What do these verses have to do with John Wesley's rule to gain all we can?

Select the one of these four verses that you find most meaningful or memorable and make a goal of memorizing it this week. To do this, recite the verse a dozen or more times each day until you internalize it. Keep the verse with you as a reminder to "gain all you can by honest industry."

Know Your Limits
Supplies: Paper, pens or markers, Bibles

Take up one or more of the following challenges:

- See who in your group can hold their breath the longest.
- Determine who can hold their hands above their head the longest.
- Determine who can hold their eyes open the longest without blinking.

Choose an activity that is appropriate for your group. The entire group can compete, or two or three can challenge each other while the rest of the group cheers them on.

Afterward, discuss:

- What would happen if you didn't stop holding your breath or holding your eyes open?
- How did you know when it was time to stop—time to put your hands down or open your eyes?

Read Proverbs 23:4. "Don't wear yourself out trying to get rich; / be smart enough to stop." Contrast this verse with the Scripture about the ant from Proverbs 6.

Working hard and earning money is good, but we need to have limits. We need to know when to stop. As a group, or in small groups of four or five, work to create a set of five to ten guidelines for making sure we don't go too far. Consider:

- When working hard has a negative effect on relationships with family and friends.
- When working hard has a negative effect on our relationship with God.
- When working hard has a negative effect on our health.
- When making money, instead of serving God and loving others, becomes our top priority.
- God's command to observe the sabbath and make time for rest (Exodus 20:8-9).

Put your list on paper and post it next to your illustration of the ant.

Menace to Society
Supplies: Paper and pens or pencils

Read the statement below about gambling.

> Gambling is a menace to society, deadly to the best interests of moral, social, economic, and spiritual life, destructive of good government and good stewardship. As an act of faith and concern, Christians should abstain from gambling and should strive to minister to those victimized by the practice.... The Church's prophetic call is to promote standards of justice and advocacy that would make it unnecessary and undesirable to

resort to commercial gambling—including public lotteries, casinos, raffles, Internet gambling, gambling with an emerging wireless technology and other games of chance—as a recreation, as an escape, or as a means of producing public revenue or funds for support of charities or government.[1] [The Social Principles of The United Methodist Church]

Discuss:

- Why do you think the statement describes gambling as a "menace to society"?
- How does the statement on gambling relate to John Wesley's rule on earning money? How is it related to Proverbs 6:6-11 (the Scripture about the ant)?

As a group, discuss some ways you agree with the statement and some ways you disagree or have questions about it.

As time permits, draft your own statement on the morality of gambling. In drafting the statement, consider the church's witness and the Scriptures you've read as a part of this study. It's fine if your statement differs considerably from the one above or if it is very similar. What's important is that you ground your statement in Scripture and in Christian tradition and witness.

More Than Money

While John Wesley had money in mind when he wrote the rule, "Gain all you can," it doesn't have to be money-specific. God has given us a host of other resources—time, talent, presence, opportunities, and so on—that we can gain.

As a group, brainstorm a list of things, other than money, that you could gain. Once you have a good list, go over each item and discuss:

- What does it mean to "gain" or earn this item?
- How can you use this item to serve God and others?

For example, you can gain the ability to play an instrument by practicing it diligently. You can then use that talent you've gained by playing the instrument in worship or by performing for persons in an assisted living facility who don't normally have the opportunity to enjoy live music. You can gain more career opportunities by working hard in school and being well-rounded. These opportunities open you up to all sorts of possibilities for doing work that serves God and God's people.

Individually, make one goal for gaining and putting to use something other than money. How can you gain talent or time or opportunity in the coming week? How can you gain in the coming year? How can you put to use what you've gained in the near future? How can you put it to use in the long term?

Discuss your goal with a partner. Check with each other during the week and next week about whether each of you has made progress toward your goal.

3.
Save All You Can

3. Save All You Can

Riches gotten quickly will dwindle,
but those who acquire them gradually
become wealthy.

—*Proverbs 13:11*

Delayed Gratification

Believe it or not, credit cards as we know them today didn't exist until the late 1950s. Before that time, consumers often made large purchases using a service called layaway. Customers who bought an item using layaway paid for it in a series of installments. Unlike other payment plans, layaway charged the consumer no interest, but the customer didn't receive the item until it was completely paid for. (Most retailers had done away with layaway by the early 2000s, but some brought it back during the most recent economic downturn.)

Buying merchandise on layaway could be frustrating, because buyers often had to wait several weeks (or longer) before they could use their new washer or dryer or coat. Layaway lacked the instant gratification that comes from buying things on credit. Yet making a purchase on layaway came with the satisfaction of having saved enough money to complete the transaction. When customers took home the couch they had purchased on layaway, they owned the couch. There would be no lingering credit card payments.

Layaway required buyers to save, to be cautious and judicious with their money in order to finish buying that appliance or suit or piece of furniture. Saving may seem out of place now that we live in a world where so much is available to us instantly and on demand, but saving money is one way that we make faithful and careful use of what God has given us. It's also the subject of John Wesley's second rule for using money.

Saving or Hoarding?

After their parents separated in 1919, Ivy League-educated brothers Homer and Langley Collyer decided to live with their mother in the family's house in Manhattan. Their mother died in 1929. Over the next few years, the Great Depression hit, bringing crime and poverty to the Collyers' neighborhood, and Homer lost his eyesight. The brothers withdrew from society, rarely leaving the house. The Collyer home became a curiosity for people in the area; rumors that the home contained valuables made it a target for robbers.

In 1947, an anonymous call to the police reported the smell of a dead body coming from the house. Police entered to discover the bodies of both brothers. Homer had died, slumped over in his chair. Langley had been crushed by a booby trap he'd set up to thwart robbery attempts. In addition to the brothers' bodies, the authorities found 130 tons of stuff, mostly junk, piled from the floor to the ceiling throughout the house. Crews removed fourteen pianos, several other musical instruments, thousands of books, stacks of old newspapers and phone books, a dressmaker's dummy, and part of a Model T Ford.[1]

The Collyers were hoarders, in the most extreme sense of the word. Compulsive hoarding is a diagnosable medical disorder and, in recent years, hoarders have become the subjects of reality television shows. We look upon hoarding as a problem, something that must be dealt with. But why do we have such a negative view of hoarding when we value saving? What is the difference?

Jesus told a parable about a wealthy man whose "land produced a bountiful crop" (Luke 12:16). This farmer, who was rich and already had plenty of food stored up, decided that he needed to build new and bigger barns to store his abundant harvest. Jesus called the man a "fool" because he would soon die, leaving his considerable stores of food for no one.

By contrast, Dorothy Ebersbach made wise use of her resources. Dorothy was born in 1915, and in the 1930s she developed a love of flying. She earned her pilot's license in 1939 and served in the Women's Airforce Service Pilots (WASP) during World War II. Following the war she graduated from the nursing school at Cleveland's prestigious Case Western Reserve University. She spent the next few decades working as a public health nurse.[2] Throughout her career, Dorothy earned a respectable salary and gave generously to her church.

When she died in 2011, she left $4.7 million to Case Western to establish the Dorothy Ebersbach Academic Center for Flight Nursing. 3 She also left a considerable gift to her church's endowment fund. The church has used this money to provide scholarships for young people who have grown up in the church as well as for seminary students (those training to go into the ministry). Unlike those who hoard money and possessions out of fear or compulsion, Dorothy saved her money and gave it purpose. Though no one would have considered her rich based on the amount of her paycheck, she undoubtedly was wise. Dorothy made sound investments and avoided frivolous purchases. Well after her death, the resources she had saved were still having a positive impact. Dorothy Ebersbach exemplified John Wesley's second financial rule, "Save all you can."

I'm a Steward, You're a Steward, We're All Stewards

Each year, when churches ask their members to consider how much money they will pledge to the church during the next twelve months, there is a lot of talk about stewardship. It would be easy for a churchgoer to get the impression that stewardship deals entirely with how much money one puts into the offering plate (or donates electronically through the church's website). But stewardship is much more than that. A "steward" is someone who manages or takes care of another person's property and resources. As God's children, we are stewards of all that God has blessed us with. This includes not only money but also time, talent, and opportunity.

Jesus told a story about a master who left his home to go on vacation and entrusted some of his property to each of three servants (Matthew 25:14-30). He gave one servant five talents, another two talents, and another one talent. (A talent was a large denomination of money.) Two of the servants invested their money, doubling its value. The master rewarded those servants by putting them in charge of more of his property. The third servant, on the other hand, buried the talent he'd been given. He was punished.

John Wesley, in his sermon "The Good Steward," advises us to be like the first two servants and make wise and productive use of the resources God has blessed us with. We can do this, in part, by following Wesley's rule to "Save all you can," setting aside money, allowing it to increase, and avoiding frivolous purchases.

According to legend, John Wesley earned 30 pounds during the first year of his ministry. He lived on 28 pounds a week, leaving him 2 pounds that he could save or give away. Before long his salary increased to 60 pounds. Since he was capable of living on 28 pounds per year, he did, leaving him 32 pounds for savings and donations. Wesley's salary continued to increase, but he was always able to live on 28 pounds. Eventually he was able to save or give away 90 percent of his income.

This story about Wesley may seem crazy. Why would we ever use such a small portion of our income for personal wants and needs? But when we consider Jesus' parable about the master and his servants, and when we remember that all our money and resources ultimately belong to God, it doesn't seem so crazy after all. We are stewards, and we have a responsibility to make wise and faithful use of all that we have.

Session 3 Activities

Check In

During the second session, you made a goal for gaining something other than money, and you discussed that goal with a partner. Talk to that partner about whether you've met that goal and, if not, what kept you from meeting it.

Planting a Vineyard

Supplies: Bibles

Read Proverbs 31:16. "She surveys a field and acquires it; / from her own resources, she plants a vineyard." In this proverb, "she" refers to the unnamed wise woman or "competent wife" (31:10). Discuss:

- What do you know about vineyards? What's the purpose of a vineyard?

The woman in this proverb doesn't purchase a vineyard that is already producing the grapes needed to make wine; rather, she's planting the vineyard from scratch. It usually takes a couple of years before grapevines are strong and mature enough to bear fruit, so the woman won't see immediate financial returns from her investment. Once the vineyard is up and going, it also will require regular upkeep. For grapevines to grow and stay healthy, someone must prune away the branches that are dead or no longer producing fruit. Planting a vineyard involves a long-term commitment. Discuss:

- When have you had to stick with or work hard at something for a long time before you enjoyed the benefits of that activity? How did you find the discipline and patience to stick with it?

John Wesley's second rule for the use of money is "Save all you can." Read "Delayed Gratification" in the chapter above, then discuss:

- How does saving money require a long-term commitment?
- What is most difficult about saving money? What pitfalls can keep you from following through on your savings goals?

Optional Activity: In honor of the wise woman in Proverbs, work with your group to plan a long-term fundraiser for your church's youth ministry or for another ministry affiliated with your congregation. Many church fundraisers are one-time events; challenge yourself to come up with a way to raise money steadily, over the long term. This might involve taking a once-a-year event—such as a chili supper or a parents' night out—and finding a way to do it in smaller but more frequent iterations. Or you might come up with something new that you could do as an ongoing fundraiser, such as creating and selling knitted items or other useful crafts. Regardless of what you choose, have a plan for how you will use the money that comes in, and let people know about that plan.

Save or Hoard?
Supplies: Bibles, paper, pens or pencils

Read "Saving or Hoarding?" in the chapter above, about the Collyer brothers. Then discuss:

- What is the difference between saving and hoarding? Is it possible to hoard money?
- How do you determine when to hold on to money and possessions and when to spend, give away, or get rid of them?
- What is dangerous or destructive about hoarding?

Read Matthew 25:14-30 and Luke 12:13-21. Jesus told both of these parables as illustrations of how we should use our money and resources. Discuss:

- In your opinion, which parable is an example of hoarding?
- Which parable is an example of saving?

Divide into two groups. Each group should take one of the two parables and rewrite it in a current-day context. Tell a story set in today's world that shows the wisdom of saving or the foolishness of hoarding. After both groups have had plenty of time to work, each group should read aloud or act out its parable.

"Riches Gotten Quickly"

Proverbs 13:11 says, "Riches gotten quickly will dwindle, / but those who acquire them gradually become wealthy." With this verse in mind, read through the following real-life stories of lottery winners.

- Lou Eisenberg won $5 million playing the lottery back in 1981. At the time, it was the biggest lottery payout in history. Prior to hitting it big, he lived on the modest sum of $250 per week. Today, more than three decades after Eisenberg became a multimillionaire, he is living below the poverty line, having lost his fortune to gambling and a series of divorce settlements.[4]

- Sharon Tirabassi grew up poor and wasn't prepared to manage the $10 million that she won in the Canadian lottery. After making some frivolous purchases, including dropping $200,000 on a souped-up Cadillac Escalade, Tirabassi ended up broke and living paycheck to paycheck.[5]

- Willie Hurt received his $3.1 million in lottery payments in annual installments of $156,000. He spent much of this money on drugs, developing a crack addiction. His marriage fell apart and he ended up charged with killing a woman in a drug-related incident.[6]

- Alex and Rhoda Toth won $13 million playing the lottery in the early 1990s. They opted to receive their winnings in 20 annual payments of $666,666. But the Toths never received the last several installments because all the money went toward paying off their considerable debts. Sadly, Alex Toth died in 2008 while awaiting trial for tax evasion.[7]

In each of the above situations, a person or couple went, literally overnight, from subsisting on a limited income to being wealthy. And in each of these situations, the wealth did not last. Discuss:

- Why do you think the people described above had so much trouble managing their money?
- If you suddenly were to come into possession of a large sum of money, how would you handle it? What would you do to make sure the money would not disappear so quickly?
- How would you advise someone who suddenly came into a large amount of money?

Savings Plan
Supplies: Index cards and pens or pencils

Privately, make a plan for saving money. Consider the following:

- How much money do you reliably bring in each week? each month?
- How much of that money can you commit to saving? Come up with a set amount or a percentage.
- Where can you put the money that you save, so you'll be able to earn money from your investment?

- Do you currently have a savings account? Do you know how much interest it earns?

If you have Internet access through a smartphone or other device, do some research on savings and money market accounts and see which ones offer the most favorable interest rates.

You might consider the 10-10-80 model. This plan suggests giving 10 percent of one's income to the church, saving another 10 percent, and having 80 percent to cover other expenses. This model is designed for adults who are paying for housing, food, transportation, and other essentials. If you don't have many necessities to pay for, you might consider increasing the amount you save or give. Regardless of what plan you come up with, record your savings goal on an index card.

The biggest obstacle to achieving your savings goals is spending money (even small amounts) on things you don't need. Make a list on your index card of five things that you are tempted to buy even though you don't need them. Keep your card with you in a wallet or purse or another place where it is readily available. Refer to it when you are tempted to spend money on one of these items.

After everyone has had a chance to make a plan and record it in private, close in prayer, thanking God for the blessings and resources we've been provided and asking God for the wisdom to be good stewards of all we've been given.

4.
Give All You Can

4. Give All You Can

Those who give generously receive more,
*   but those who are stingy with what is*
*   appropriate will grow needy.*
Generous persons will prosper; those who
*   refresh others will themselves be refreshed.*
                                    —*Proverbs 11:24-25*

She reaches out to the needy;
*   she stretches out her hands to the poor.*
                                    —*Proverbs 31:26*

A Soul for 62 Cents

If you ever watched the cartoon *SpongeBob SquarePants*, you're familiar with Eugene Krabs, the miserly manager of the Krusty Krab restaurant and the title character's boss. Mr. Krabs is a penny pincher. In one episode, "Born Again Krabs," SpongeBob is working the grill at the Krusty Krab and discovers an old, rotten burger patty under the grill. Mr. Krabs, ever concerned about food costs, tells SpongeBob not to put another burger on the grill until they sell the rotten one. When Squidward, SpongeBob's coworker, suggests that the burger is not fit to be eaten, Mr. Krabs tries to prove him wrong by taking a bite—a bite that puts him in the hospital.

In the hospital the ghost of the Flying Dutchman visits Mr. Krabs to take him away to Davy Jones' Locker, an old sailor's expression for the bottom of the sea and an undesirable afterlife location in the *SpongeBob* universe. Eventually SpongeBob intervenes on behalf of his boss, vouching for his generosity. The Dutchman tests this, asking Mr. Krabs to choose between SpongeBob's immortal soul and the money in the Dutchman's pocket, 62 cents. Mr. Krabs chooses the money, condemning SpongeBob.

Despite the dark overtones, the story has a happy ending. Ultimately the Flying Dutchman, who cannot bear to spend eternity with someone as annoying as SpongeBob, returns the little yellow fry cook to the realm of the living.[1]

Most of us have met a Mr. Krabs. He isn't interested in using money to accomplish some purpose; he just wants to have it. Krabs doesn't save money; he hoards it. Jesus addressed those who take such an approach to money and to life—those who would sell a friend for 62 cents:

> "All who want to save their lives will lose them. But all who lose their lives because of me and because of the good news will save them. Why would people gain the whole world but lose their lives?" (Mark 8:35-36)

A Tenth-Part

Thus far in this study, we've looked at earning and saving. Wisely earning and saving can put a lot of money in our bank accounts, but what's the point? What's the purpose of acquiring all that wealth? Are we to become like Mr. Krabs, so obsessed with gaining and holding onto money that we sacrifice our relationships? The witness of Scripture and from Christian thinkers throughout history tells us that the purpose of hard work and wise investments is generosity. We gain and save money and other resources so we can give back to God and to those who need it most.

The idea that we should give away a portion of our earnings shows up early in Scripture. The law that God gave to the people of Israel included instructions to give a "tenth-part" gift from their harvest as an offering to God. This charge to give a tenth or "tithe" comes up several times in Scripture. In the Book of Malachi, likely written when the Jewish people were resettling their homeland after years of exile in Babylon, God tells the people that withholding their tithe is the equivalent of robbery. By not giving a full tenth of their crop, they were deceiving God and denying food to the storehouses that offered food security to the entire nation. This teaching about tithes is grounded in the truth that all that we have ultimately belongs to God and that we are only stewards of that which God provides.

When we think of our money and possessions as entirely our own, it's easy to be stingy. When we think of ourselves as God's stewards, our attitude changes.

"Employ Whatever God Has Entrusted You With"

John Wesley's third financial rule is "Give all you can." Toward the end of his sermon, "The Use of Money," he said, "Employ whatever God has entrusted you with, in doing good, all possible good, in every possible kind and degree to the household of faith."[2] In other words, as much as you can, use all your God-given resources, including money, to benefit God's people. While God's law in Scripture directs us to give 10 percent of our income, generosity is about more than just donating a percentage.

During his final week in Jerusalem, Jesus went to the Temple with his disciples and watched as visitors added their donations to the Temple treasury. They saw a widow give two copper coins, a meager amount that seemed worthless in comparison to the donations of wealthier visitors. But Jesus understood that what the widow had given was worth far more than the other gifts because those two copper coins represented "everything she had to live on" (Luke 21:4).

The Apostle Paul urged the Christians in the Greek city of Corinth to be generous with their money and resources. But instead of suggesting a percentage they should donate he said, "Everyone should give whatever they have decided in their heart. They shouldn't give with hesitation or because of pressure. God loves a cheerful giver" (2 Corinthians 9:7).

When we give all that we can from what "God has entrusted" us with, we should remember the example of the widow and the teaching of Paul. We shouldn't think of giving gifts as a requirement, something we can do and then check off. We shouldn't give simply because we feel that we have to; and we shouldn't stop giving just because we hit the 10 percent mark. The value of our gifts can't necessarily be measured in dollars and cents. Rather, it is measured by the spirit in which the gift was given and the sacrifice that the gift required.

Session 4 Activities

Check In

During the previous session you made a savings plan. Talk with a partner about whether during the previous week you've been able to implement that plan and how, during the coming weeks, you will follow through on it.

For a Million Dollars
Supplies: Bibles

Group members should try to think of one thing they would be willing to do for a million dollars that others in the group might refuse to do. Give everyone a couple of minutes to come up with an idea. Then have each person say what he or she would do. After each example, the other members of the group should vote on whether they'd be willing to do the same thing for a million-dollar prize. Determine which million-dollar task is most popular and which task the members of the group would be least likely to do. Then discuss:

- What is the limit of what you would do for a million dollars?
- If the amount of money were increased (say, to a billion dollars), would you be willing to do more?

Read Matthew 16:24-26. Discuss:

- Think about the things you were willing to do for a million dollars or more. Would you consider any of these things immoral or detrimental to your relationship with God or others?
- What, if anything, might you lose by doing one of these tasks for a million dollars?
- What sacrifices might we have to make to "find" our lives in Christ?

Give Cheerfully
Supplies: Bibles

John Wesley's third rule for the use of money is "Give all you can." All the earning and saving we discussed in previous sessions has a purpose. We can offer God the resources we save, and we can use them for the benefit of God's people.

The 10-10-80 plan, which we looked at in the previous session, is a popular model for faithfully managing money. The first 10 refers to the percent of our income we should give away; the second 10 refers to the percent we should save; and the 80 refers to the rest, which we may use at our discretion, provided that we make wise choices.

Read and discuss these Scriptures:

- Leviticus 27:30. Some translations say "tithe" and some say "tenth-part gifts." In either case, the passage is talking about 10 percent of a family's harvest.
- Malachi 3:8-10. What does this Scripture say about not giving a full tenth to God?

Both of these Scriptures instruct us to give a tenth of our income to God. But in a letter to the church in Corinth, the Apostle Paul has a slightly different take: "Everyone should give whatever they have decided in their heart. They shouldn't give with hesitation or because of pressure. God loves a cheerful giver" (2 Corinthians 9: 7). Discuss:

- What do you think Paul means by "a cheerful giver"?
- What do Paul's words in these verses say about how much of our income we should give?

- Paul says, "Everyone should give whatever they have decided in their heart." Can we "decide" to give less than 10 percent? Why or why not?

With a partner, talk about a time when giving generously made you happy. Talk about how you felt before giving the gift or donation. (Were you reluctant? Were you apprehensive? Did you give of your own volition, or did someone pressure you?) Then discuss how you felt after giving the gift or making the donation. (What was most satisfying about the gift? Did you have any regrets?)

Clean Out the Pantry
Supplies: Bibles, five or ten canned or boxed foods per person

Each person in your group should bring in a variety of canned and boxed foods from home. If possible, bring some items that your family eats frequently and some that your family rarely eats or might never eat.

Read Leviticus 23:22. The practice described, in which poor people and immigrants picked crops that were left for them by farmers, was called gleaning. Discuss:

- How do we set aside food today so it can be gleaned by those who need it most?
- Aside from food, what other things can we consider setting aside for people in need?

As a group, set out all your foods and label them with sticky notes. (You can just label them by number or letter.) Imagine that your church or school is having a food drive. Each person should identify the five items that he or she would most likely donate to the food drive. (If you have enough items, each person should select ten; instead of bringing in cans and boxes, you could just take pictures.)

All the group members should say which items they selected and why. They should consider whether the items chosen were ones that their family would be likely to eat or ones that might never leave the pantry. Discuss:

- Is there a difference between donating canned foods that you would like to eat and donating canned foods that you don't care for?
- Aside from canned goods, what are some other items that you might have opportunities to donate?
- When you have chances to donate clothes, old toys, electronics, or other possessions, how do you determine what you are willing to give and what you cannot part with?

Don't Stop With Money

Supplies: A markerboard and markers, a large sheet of paper, markers (or colored pencils or crayons)

When we think of giving, we usually think of money and possessions. But we can give much more.

As a group, brainstorm things other than money and possessions that one could offer to God or donate for the good of others (such as time, presence, or specific talents and abilities). List these on a markerboard.

Everybody should choose one of the things listed. One person could offer the gift of presence to a peer or church member who is hurting; one could offer a talent for singing or playing an instrument to use in worship; one could use leadership abilities to organize a fundraiser for a mission or ministry.

As a group, create a poster or mural representing these gifts. Group members should draw on the poster or mural something representing the gift or donation they could give. They can draw a symbol of the gift, or they may draw themselves giving the gift. If time permits, coordinate your poster or mural so that all the pictures flow together.

Display your finished mural in your meeting space as a reminder of the ways you can "Give all you can."

Wisdom From a Widow

Supplies: Bibles, index cards, pens or pencils

Read Luke 21:1-4, in which Jesus watches as visitors—including a poor widow—add their offerings to the temple treasury. Discuss:

- Why did Jesus consider the widow's gift so valuable?
- What sacrifice did the widow make?
- What can we learn from the widow's example?
- How does it hurt to make sacrifices? What is satisfying about making sacrifices?

Think of one thing you could donate that you don't absolutely need but that someone else may find useful. Try to select something that would be difficult to part with and that could be more valuable to the recipient than it is to you.

Take a few minutes to think it over, then reveal to a partner what you plan to give away. During the coming week, donate the item to an appropriate agency or program (such as a shelter, a toy drive, an organization that restores electronics for low-income families, or the Salvation Army). You and your partner should keep tabs on one another (by texting or messaging through social media) to make sure that each of you follows through on the commitment.

Finally, set a goal for giving to your congregation. The goal might include an amount of money you could give weekly or monthly as well as how you will offer your talents, presence, prayers, and other resources. Record the goal on an index card that you can keep in your wallet, purse, Bible, or other important place. Refer to it the next time your congregation asks for pledges or has a stewardship campaign.

After everyone has had time to write down and think about their goal for giving, close with prayer, asking God for the courage to give generously, especially when it requires making sacrifices.

Notes

Chapter 1. We Don't Need More Money; We Need Wisdom

1. John Wesley, "The Use of Money," Sermon 50, http://www
    .umcmission.org/Find-Resources/John-Wesley-Sermons
    /Sermon-50-The-Use-of-Money, III, 1.

Chapter 2. Earn All You Can.

1. The Social Principles of The United Methodist Church,
    The Economic Community, *The Book of Discipline of
    The United Methodist Church* (Nashville: The United
    Methodist Publishing House, 2012), ¶ 163.G.

Chapter 3. Save All You Can

1. Thomas Cunningham, "Collyer's Mansion Conditions,"
    Firehouse, published December 22, 2003, accessed February
    24, 2015, http://www.firehouse.com/news/10529720
    /collyers-mansion-conditions.
2. "Dorothy Ebersbach Bio," *Flight Nursing Program: Frances
    Payne Bolton School of Nursing at Case Western Reserve
    University*, accessed February 24, 2015, http://flightnurse
    .case.edu/ebersbach.shtm.

3. "Ebersbach Estate Trustees Announce $4.7 Million Total Gifts to FPB," *Flight Nursing Program: Frances Payne Bolton School of Nursing at Case Western Reserve University*, accessed Fenruary 24, 2015, http://fpb.case.edu /News/ebersbachgift.shtm#.VO0gTShlxcQ.

4. Rob Kramer, "10 Lottery Winners Who Went Broke—Lou Eisenberg," *The Richest*, published July 15, 2014, accessed Febraury 24, 2015, http://www.therichest.com/rich-list /poorest-list/10-lottery-winners-who-went-broke/3/.

5. Rob Kramer, "10 Lottery Winners Who Went Broke— Sharon Terabassi," *The Richest*, published July 15, 2014, accessed Febraury 24, 2015, http://www.therichest.com /rich-list/poorest-list/10-lottery-winners-who-went -broke/5/.

6. Rob Kramer, "10 Lottery Winners Who Went Broke— Willie Hurt, "*The Richest*, published July 15, 2014, accessed Febraury 24, 2015, http://www.therichest.com/rich-list /poorest-list/10-lottery-winners-who-went-broke/7/.

7. Keith Morelli, "Lottery winner Toth goes from riches to rags," *The Tampa Tribune*, published September 24, 2010, accessed Febraury 24, 2015, http://tbo.com/events/lottery -winner-toth-goes-from-rags-to-riches-to-rags-28855.

Chapter 4. Give All You Can.

1. "SpongeBob SquarePants" Born Again Krabs/I Had an Accident (TV Episode 2003)," *Internet Movie Database*, accessed February 24, 2015, http://www.imdb.com/title /tt0707288/plotsummary?ref_=tt_ov_pl.

2. John Wesley, "The Use of Money," Sermon 50, http://www .umcmission.org/Find-Resources/John-Wesley-Sermons /Sermon-50-The-Use-of-Money, III, 7.